Happy TRAVELS!

"From the hills to the rivers; horse farms to coal fields; caves to historic homes and *every point of interest* in between, Michael is your perfect and ultimate tour guide for the Bluegrass State. Put *this book* on your definitive bucket list!"

- Kenny Rice, NBC Sports

100 Ways to Have a Real Kentucky Experience

The Kentucky Bucket List

Michael Crisp

The Kentucky Bucket List

100 Ways to Have a Real Kentucky Experience

Michael Crisp

REMIX BOOKS

Published in Georgetown, KY

United States of America

Remix Books
PO Box 1303
Georgetown, KY 40324

www.kentuckybucketlist.com

Layout by Scott Hall

Cover Design by Kevin Kifer
www.k2-technology.com

ISBN 978-1-4675-4906-6

First Edition

legal disclaimer

Henry Clay, famous American statesman who called Lexington his home. *Photo courtesy the Library of Congress.*

dedication

For Conner and Ryder. May you find many adventures in your lives, and may many adventures also find you.

bucket list:

a number of experiences or achievements that a person hopes to have or accomplish during their lifetime.

Courtesy of the Oxford American Dictionary

I'm very proud to call Kentucky my home. I moved here with my family in the spring of 1974, and since then I've been fortunate enough to travel all over the state and enjoy a great deal of amazing experiences. Putting together this list of wonderful things to do in Kentucky is definitely one of them.

In writing this book, I wanted to combine all of the quintessential "things to do" in Kentucky with some of the more obscure experiences that the state has to offer. Sure, almost everyone in the world is familiar with the Kentucky Derby or Mammoth Cave, but how many people know about the world's smallest church (in Crestview Hills) or Herry the Hairless Loch Herrington Monster (in Harrodsburg)? With that being said, I knew a "bucket list" book was needed in order to help inspire a series of adventures for everyone who loves the bluegrass state and everything it has to offer.

While writing this book, I came across a handful of items that helped me in my research. The *Lexington Herald Leader* published an article on September 22, 2011 which featured their own "bucket list" of places to visit and things to do throughout the commonwealth. Also helpful were the books *Kentucky Curiosities* by Vince Staten and Liz Baldi, as well as *Weird Kentucky*, written by Jeffrey Scott Holland.

One of the biggest inspirations for this book is my good friend, David Sloan. David is an author (and all-around renaissance man) who resides in Key West, Florida, and he has penned several books over the last few years. His latest book, *The Key West Bucket List*, has met with great success, including being featured on The Travel Channel.

what to expect

1. No Instruction Manual:
This book isn't an instructional guidebook that tells you what to do and how to do it. The object here is for you to seek out each of the items in this book and then enjoy these experiences on your own.

2. Adventure and Challenge:
Some of the items on this list are easy to accomplish, some are more difficult, and others are downright close to impossible. Don't worry - no one is watching you or grading your performance. Take each adventure one by one, at your own pace, and you will get the most out of this book.

3. Inspiration:
I've often been accused of being a "know-it-all" (especially after I've had a few cold beverages), but I'm definitely not a fountain of wisdom. That's why I called in the experts. Mark Twain, Helen Keller, Edgar Allan Poe, and Thomas Edison are all contributors with quotes that lend a deeper meaning to each adventure.

4. Satisfaction:

Whether you fill out the list at the end of this book with a fat red pen, or you take each of these journeys in your mind from the comfort of your favorite chair, this book should leave you with a profound sense of satisfaction. You will have so much fun with this book that you'll probably feel like sharing your own thoughts and stories with others. Feel free to visit www.kentuckybucketlist.com to share your musings, experiences, photos, and new additions to the list.

Enjoy.
Michael Crisp

"It is only in adventure that some people succeed in knowing themselves - in finding themselves."

- Andre Gide

1

attend the Kentucky Derby
Churchill Downs, Louisville, Kentucky

"Horse sense is the thing a horse has which keeps it from betting on people."

- **W.C. Fields**

2

drink moonshine from a mason jar
almost anywhere, but preferably eastern Kentucky

"Alcohol may be man's worst enemy, but the Bible says love your enemy."

- Frank Sinatra

3

sleep in a houseboat on Lake Cumberland
Somerset, Kentucky

"Rivers, ponds, lakes and streams - they all have different names, but they all contain water. Just as religions do - they all contain truth."

- Muhammad Ali

4

ride the rails on My Old Kentucky Dinner Train

Bardstown, Kentucky

"Truth gets well if she is run over by a locomotive, while error dies of lockjaw if she scratches her finger."

- William C. Bryant

5

tour the Portal 31 coal mine
Lynch, Kentucky

"Deep into that darkness peering, long I stood there, wondering, fearing, doubting, dreaming dreams no mortal ever dared to dream before."

- Edgar Allan Poe

6

visit the grave of Daniel Boone

Frankfort Cemetery, Frankfort, Kentucky

"All you need for happiness is a good gun, a good horse, and a good wife."

- Daniel Boone

7

discover Swift's Silver Mine
Wolfe County, Kentucky

"There is more treasure in books than in all the pirate's loot on Treasure Island."

- **Walt Disney**

8

see the birthplace
of Abraham Lincoln
Hodgenville, Kentucky

"Those who deny freedom to others deserve it not for themselves."

*- **Abraham Lincoln***

9

eat goetta sausage for breakfast
Covington, Kentucky

"I come from a family where gravy is considered a beverage."

- ***Erma Bombeck***

10

listen to a political speech at the Fancy Farm picnic
Fancy Farm, Kentucky

"A fool and his money are soon elected."

- Will Rogers

11

scuba dive at the Falling Rock Quarry
La Grange, Kentucky

"Look deep into nature, and then you will understand everything better."

- Albert Einstein

12

sing *My Old Kentucky Home*
almost anywhere, but preferably
Bardstown, Kentucky

"Music is forever; music should grow and mature with you, following you right on up until you die."

- Paul Simon

13

walk across the West Prestonsburg bridge
Prestonsburg, Kentucky

"Never go on trips with anyone you do not love."

- Ernest Hemingway

14

visit the National Quilt Museum
Paducah, Kentucky

"A gentle heart is tied with an easy thread."

- George Herbert

15

explore Mammoth Cave
Mammoth Cave, Kentucky

"Everything has its wonders, even darkness and silence, and I learn, whatever state I might be in, therein to be content."

- Helen Keller

Mammoth Cave. *Photo courtesy the Library of Congress.*

16

visit a town with an unusual name

almost anywhere, but definitely
Possum Trot, Monkey's Eyebrow,
Bugtussle, Cut Shin, Rabbit Hash,
or Gravel Switch

*"Happiness is having a large, loving, caring,
close-knit family in another city."*

- George Burns

17

watch a Civil War reenactment
almost anywhere, but preferably
Perryville, Kentucky

*"In peace, sons bury their fathers. In war,
fathers bury their sons."*

- Herodotus

18

eat fried chicken at Claudia Sanders' Dinner House
Shelbyville, Kentucky

"Don't be against things so much as for things."

> *- Colonel Harland Sanders*

19

attend a UK basketball game
Rupp Arena
Lexington, Kentucky

"I'd rather be the most hated winning coach in the country than the most popular losing one."

- Adolph Rupp

20

plan a heist
United States Bullion Depository
Fort Knox, Kentucky

"I have always felt that if a man gives you a solid gold key to his door he is entitled to the courtesy of a visit."

- ***Hedy Lamarr***

Cumberland Falls. *Photo courtesy the Library of Congress.*

21

see a moonbow at Cumberland Falls
Corbin, Kentucky

"Three things cannot be long hidden: the sun, the moon, and the truth."

- ***Buddha***

22

eat a hot brown at the Brown Hotel
Louisville, Kentucky

"Older people shouldn't eat health food - they need all the preservatives they can get."

- Robert Orben

23

take a picture of
the castle
Versailles, Kentucky

"Even castles made of sand, fall into the sea, eventually."

- ***Jimi Hendrix***

24

enjoy the view at Natural Bridge
Slade, Kentucky

"We build too many walls and not enough bridges."

- Isaac Newton

Natural Bridge. *Photo courtesy the Library of Congress.*

25

tour the
Corvette Museum
Bowling Green, Kentucky

"When we get to the track, we're basically turned loose to the masses. And you'd better be willing to deal with that politely, slightly, lightly all nightly - whatever it takes."

- Darrell Waltrip

26

spend the night at the Waverly Hills Sanitorium
Louisville, Kentucky

"Fear makes strangers of people who would be friends."

- Shirley MacLaine

27

have dinner at the Bucket List Bar & Grill
Somerset, Kentucky

"I have friends in overalls whose friendship I would not swap for the favor of the kings of the world."

- Thomas Edison

28

visit Shaker Village
Harrodsburg, Kentucky

"Technology is nothing. What's important is that you have a faith in people, that they're basically good and smart, and if you give them tools, they'll do wonderful things with them."

- Steve Jobs

29

listen to a bluegrass music jam session

almost anywhere, but preferably on a front porch

"Bluegrass has brought more people together and made more friends than any music in the world."

- Bill Monroe

30

see the statue of Man O' War
Kentucky Horse Park
Lexington, Kentucky

"Excellence is to do a common thing in an uncommon way."

- Booker T. Washington

31

visit the grave of Randall McCoy
Hatfields & McCoys Walking Tour
Pikeville, Kentucky

"Family is not an important thing. It's everything."

- Michael J. Fox

32

drink an Ale-8-One
almost anywhere, but preferably
in Winchester, Kentucky

"The remedy for thirst? It is the opposite of the one for dog bite: run always after a dog, he'll never bite you; drink always before thirst, and it will never overtake you."

- Francois Rabelais

33

take a cruise on the
Belle of Louisville
Louisville, Kentucky

"Ideas, like large rivers, never have just one source."

- Willy Ley

34

attend the
Rosemary Clooney
Music Festival
Maysville, Kentucky

"When you're young you believe it when people tell you how good you are. And that's the danger, you inhale. Everyone will tell you you're a genius, which you are not, and if you understand that, you win."

- George Clooney

35

dress up and go to Keeneland
Lexington, Kentucky

"Fashion fades, only style remains the same."

- Coco Chanel

36

go fishing at Land Between the Lakes
Golden Pond, Kentucky

"If people concentrated on the really important things in life, there'd be a shortage of fishing poles."

- Doug Larson

37

visit Loretta Lynn's Homeplace at Butcher Holler
Van Lear, Kentucky

"In the long run you make your own luck - good, bad, or indifferent."

- Loretta Lynn

38

spend the afternoon at Florence Mall
Florence, Kentucky

"Whoever said money can't buy happiness simply didn't know where to go shopping."

- Bo Derek

39

buy produce from a roadside stand
almost anywhere, but preferably
in Barbourville, Kentucky

*"I think this is what hooks one to gardening:
it is the closest one can come to being
present at creation."*

- Phyllis Theroux

A spring warbler. *Photo courtesy the Library of Congress.*

40

sight a spring warbler at Jenny Wiley State Park
Prestonsburg, Kentucky

"Use what talents you possess; the woods would be very silent if no birds sang there except those that sang best."

- Henry Van Dyke

41

see an exotic animal

Louisville Zoo
Louisville, Kentucky

"Animals are reliable, many full of love, true in their affections, predictable in their actions, grateful and loyal. Difficult standards for people to live up to."

- Alfred A. Montapert

42

visit the Mary Todd Lincoln House
Lexington, Kentucky

"Tough girls come from New York. Sweet girls, they're from Georgia. But us Kentucky girls, we have fire and ice in our blood. We can ride horses, be a debutante, throw left hooks, and drink with the boys. And if we have an opinion, you know you're gonna hear about it."

- Ashley Judd

43

share silence
with a monk
The Abbey of Gethsemani
New Haven, Kentucky

"A happy life must be to a great extent a quiet life, for it is only in an atmosphere of quiet that true joy dare live."

- Bertrand Russell

44

eat a slice of
Derby-Pie®
From Kern's Kitchen,
Louisville, Kentucky

"I don't want to spend my life not having good food going into my pie hole. That hole was made for pies."

- Paula Deen

45

visit the
Creation Museum
with your family
Petersburg, Kentucky

"I cannot think that we are useless or God would not have created us. There is one God looking down on us all. We are all the children of one God. The sun, the darkness, the winds are all listening to what we have to say."

- *Geronimo*

46

spot a celebrity
almost anywhere, but preferably
in Midway, Kentucky

*"How do I stay healthy and boyishly
handsome? It's simple: I drink the blood of
young runaways."*

*- **William Shatner***

47

feed the ducks at Noble Park
Paducah, Kentucky

"American society is a sort of flat, fresh-water pond which absorbs silently, without reaction, anything which is thrown in it."

- Henry B. Adams

48

go barhopping with friends at Fourth Street Live
Louisville, Kentucky

"I hate to advocate drugs, alcohol, violence, or insanity to anyone, but they've always worked for me."

- Hunter S. Thompson

49

visit the home of Henry Clay

Ashland: The Henry Clay Estate
Lexington, Kentucky

"Of all the properties which belong to honorable men, not one is so highly prized as that of character."

- Henry Clay

50

see a ghost at
Bobby Mackey's
Music World
Wilder, Kentucky

"Of all ghosts, the ghosts of our old loves are the worst."

- Arthur Conan Doyle

51

eat beer cheese at Hall's on the River
Winchester, Kentucky

"Age is something that doesn't matter, unless you are a cheese."

- Billie Burke

52

wear a "Gettin' Lucky in Kentucky" t-shirt

almost anywhere, but preferably in a very public place

"I feel that luck is preparation meeting opportunity."

- Oprah Winfrey

53

watch a show at the Pioneer Playhouse
Danville, Kentucky

"I pretty much try to stay in a constant state of confusion just because of the expression it leaves on my face."

- Johnny Depp

54

sit inside the
Cane Ridge
Meeting House
Paris, Kentucky

"I like the silent church before the service begins, better than any preaching."

- Ralph Waldo Emerson

55

swing a bat at the Louisville Slugger Museum
Louisville, Kentucky

"Baseball is the only field of endeavor where a man can succeed three times out of ten and be considered a good performer."

- *Ted Williams*

56

camp out at
Red River Gorge
Slade, Kentucky

*"The best remedy for those who are afraid,
lonely or unhappy is to go outside,
somewhere they can be quiet, alone with
the heavens, nature and God. Because
only then does one feel that all is as it
should be."*

- Anne Frank

57

use the outhouse at Penn's Store
Gravel Switch, Kentucky

"I grew up with six brothers. That's how I learned to dance - waiting for the bathroom."

- Bob Hope

58

spend a few minutes in jail
The 1811 Augusta Jail
Augusta, Kentucky

"A pedestal is as much a prison as any small, confined space."

- Gloria Steinem

59

see "the procession that never moves"
Tomb of Henry Wooldridge
Mayfield, Kentucky

"If you're poor and you do something stupid, you're nuts. If you're rich and you do something stupid, you're eccentric."

— **Bobby Heenan**

60

take a trip on the Bourbon Trail

Four Roses, Lawrenceburg
Wild Turkey, Lawrenceburg
Heaven Hill, Bardstown
Jim Beam, Clermont
Maker's Mark, Loretto
Woodford Reserve, Versailles

"I like whiskey. I always did, and that is why I never drink it."

- Robert E. Lee

61

watch a race at the Kentucky Speedway
Sparta, Kentucky

"Life is like a ten speed bicycle. Most of us have gears we never use."

- Charles Schulz

62

take a ride on the Valley View Ferry
Nicholasville, Kentucky and Richmond, Kentucky

"To me, if life boils down to one thing it's movement. To live is to keep moving."

- Jerry Seinfeld

63

visit the Muhammad Ali Museum
Louisville, Kentucky

"Like a lot of things in life, when you put the gloves on, it's better to give than to receive."

- Sugar Ray Leonard

64

sleep in a teepee
Wigwam Village Motel,
Cave City, Kentucky

"Sleep is the best meditation."

- Dalai Lama

65

attend the Garrard County Tobacco Cutting Festival
Lancaster, Kentucky

"There's nothing quite like tobacco. It's the passion of decent folk, and whoever lives without tobacco doesn't deserve to live."

- *Moliere*

66

enjoy a concert at Renfro Valley
Renfro Valley, Kentucky

"Country music is the people's music. It just speaks about real life and about truth and it tells things how they really are."

- Faith Hill

67

savor a
Blue Monday
cream candy
Ruth Hunt Candy Company
Mt. Sterling, Kentucky

"A wise woman puts a grain of sugar into everything she says to a man, and takes a grain of salt with everything he says to her."

- Helen Rowland

68

play a round of golf at Valhalla
Valhalla Golf Club
Louisville, Kentucky

"If you think it's hard to meet new people, try picking up the wrong golf ball."

- ***Jack Lemmon***

69

go to a party thrown by Russ Renbarger
almost anywhere, but preferably
Louisville or Lexington

*"Why is partying and having a good time
bad?"*

- Tara Reid

70

touch the pillars of Stonehenge
Kentucky's Stonehenge
Munfordville, Kentucky

"Let others praise ancient times; I am glad I was born in these."

- ***Ovid***

71

spend a day at Newport on the Levee
Newport, Kentucky

"The river flows at its own sweet will, but the flood is bound in the two banks. If it were not thus bound, its freedom would be wasted."

- Vinoba Bhave

72

see the Palisades
Jim Beam Nature Preserve
Nicholasville, Kentucky

"You've got to jump off cliffs and build your wings on the way down."

- ***Ray Bradbury***

73

go birdwatching at the Audubon State Park
Henderson, Kentucky

"You can observe a lot just by watching."

- Yogi Berra

74

enjoy a bourbon ball
Rebecca-Ruth Candy Company, Frankfort, Kentucky

"Candy is dandy but liquor is quicker."

- Ogden Nash

75

drive slowly under a covered bridge

Goddard Bridge
Flemingsburg, Kentucky

"Two roads diverged in a wood and I - I took the one less traveled by, and that has made all the difference."

- Robert Frost

76

see the Jefferson Davis monument

Jefferson Davis State Historic Site
Fairview, Kentucky

"I've never seen a monument erected to a pessimist."

- Paul Harvey

77

admire a painting
in the
Speed Art Museum
Louisville, Kentucky

"Love of beauty is taste. The creation of beauty is art."

- ***Ralph Waldo Emerson***

78

go kayaking in the Rockcastle River
Billows, Kentucky

"Being an old maid is like death by drowning, a really delightful sensation after you cease to struggle."

- *Edna Ferber*

79

tour a horse farm
almost anywhere in
central Kentucky

*"Old minds are like horses; you must
exercise them if you wish to keep them in
working order."*

- *John Adams*

80

drive by the Mother Goose House at night

Hazard, Kentucky

"All children are artists. The problem is how to remain an artist once he grows up."

- Pablo Picasso

81

become a
Kentucky Colonel
State Capitol Building
Frankfort, Kentucky

"It is not titles that honor men, but men that honor titles."

- Niccolo Machiavelli

82

tour the Toyota plant
Georgetown, Kentucky

"I know a lot about cars, man. I can look at any car's headlights and tell you exactly which way it's coming."

- *Mitch Hedberg*

83

search for Herry the Hairless Loch Herrington Monster
Harrodsburg, Kentucky

"When I die, I'm leaving my body to science fiction."

- Steven Wright

84

make a mint julep
almost anywhere, but preferably
in the company of good friends

"It is the destiny of mint to be crushed."

*- **Waverley Lewis
Root***

85

visit the world's smallest church
Monte Cassino Chapel
Crestview Hills, Kentucky

"Be faithful in small things because it is in them that your strength lies."

- ***Mother Teresa***

86

pig out at the International Bar-B-Q Festival
Owensboro, Kentucky

"A good upbringing means not that you won't spill sauce on the tablecloth, but that you won't notice it when someone else does."

- Anton Chekhov

87

touch the walls
of the
Fitchburg Furnace
Irvine, Kentucky

"Everything has its limit - iron ore cannot be educated into gold."

- Mark Twain

88

visit the
Harland Sanders
Cafe and Museum
Corbin, Kentucky

"Hard work spotlights the character of people: some turn up their sleeves, some turn up their noses, and some don't turn up at all."

- Sam Ewing

89

pay your respects
at the Vietnam
Veterans Memorial
Frankfort, Kentucky

"A man's country is not a certain area of land, of mountains, rivers, and woods, but it is a principle and patriotism is loyalty to that principle."

- ***George William Curtis***

90

climb Pilot Rocks
Hopkinsville, Kentucky

"After climbing a great hill, one only finds that there are many more hills to climb."

- Nelson Mandela

91

see a movie at the Kentucky Theatre
Lexington, Kentucky

"You know what your problem is? You haven't seen enough movies. All of life's riddles are answered in the movies."

- Steve Martin

92

attend the Kentucky State Fair
Louisville, Kentucky

"If you ever start feeling like you have the goofiest, craziest, most dysfunctional family in the world, all you have to do is go to a state fair. Because five minutes at the fair, you'll be going, 'you know, we're alright. We are dang near royalty.'"

- Jeff Foxworthy

93

shoot a gun
almost anywhere, but preferably in the woods

"The perils of duck hunting are great - especially for the duck."

- Walter Cronkite

94

explore the
Cumberland Gap
Middlesboro, Kentucky

"In every walk with nature one receives far more than he seeks."

- John Muir

95

buy something that a Kentuckian made

almost anything, but preferably something you can display in your home

"A man who works with his hands is a laborer; a man who works with his hands and his brain is a craftsman; but a man who works with his hands and his brain and his heart is an artist."

- Louis Nizer

96

get your wings in a flight simulator
Highlands Museum
Ashland, Kentucky

"Pilots take no special joy in walking. Pilots like flying."

- ***Neil Armstrong***

97

walk the grounds of Old Fort Harrod
Harrodsburg, Kentucky

"Civilization began the first time an angry person cast a word instead of a rock."

- Sigmund Freud

98

see a model t
Swope's Cars of Yesteryear
Museum
Elizabethtown, Kentucky

"It is easily overlooked that what is now called vintage was once brand new."

- Tony Visconti

99

see a bank robbed by Jesse James
Logan County Museum
(formerly Southern Deposit Bank)
Russellville, Kentucky

"Love is the ultimate outlaw. It just won't adhere to any rules. The most any of us can do is sign on as its accomplice."

- Tom Robbins

100

share a story
with the author of
this book
almost anywhere, but preferably
where cold beverages are served

*"There is nothing on this earth more to be
prized than true friendship."*

- Thomas Aquinas

i did it

Check off your accomplishments with the writing utensil of your choice:

☐ 1. attend the Kentucky Derby
☐ 2. drink moonshine from a mason jar
☐ 3. sleep in a houseboat on Lake Cumberland
☐ 4. ride the rails on My Old Kentucky Dinner Train
☐ 5. tour the Portal 31 coal mine
☐ 6. visit the grave of Daniel Boone
☐ 7. discover Swift's Silver Mine
☐ 8. see the birthplace of Abraham Lincoln
☐ 9. eat goetta sausage for breakfast
☐ 10. listen to a political speech at the Fancy Farm Picnic
☐ 11. scuba dive at the Falling Rock Quarry
☐ 12. sing *My Old Kentucky Home*
☐ 13. walk across the West Prestonsburg bridge
☐ 14. Visit the National Quilt Museum
☐ 15. explore Mammoth Cave
☐ 16. visit a town with an unusual name
☐ 17. watch a Civil War reenactment
☐ 18. eat fried chicken at Claudia Sanders' Dinner House
☐ 19. attend a UK basketball game
☐ 20. plan a heist

- [ ] 21. see a moonbow at Cumberland Falls
- [ ] 22. eat a hot brown at the Brown Hotel
- [ ] 23. take a picture of the castle
- [ ] 24. enjoy the view at Natural Bridge
- [ ] 25. tour the Corvette Museum
- [ ] 26. spend the night at the Waverly Hills Sanitorium
- [ ] 27. have dinner at the Bucket List Bar & Grill
- [ ] 28. visit Shaker Village
- [ ] 29. listen to a bluegrass music jam session
- [ ] 30. see the statue of Man O' War
- [ ] 31. visit the grave of Randall McCoy
- [ ] 32. drink an Ale-8-One
- [ ] 33. take a cruise on the Belle of Louisville
- [ ] 34. attend the Rosemary Clooney Music Festival
- [ ] 35. dress up and go to Keeneland
- [ ] 36. go fishing at Land Between the Lakes
- [ ] 37. visit Loretta Lynn's homeplace at Butcher Holler
- [ ] 38. spend the afternoon at Florence Mall
- [ ] 39. buy produce from a roadside stand
- [ ] 40. sight a spring warbler at Jenny Wiley State Park
- [ ] 41. see an exotic animal
- [ ] 42. visit the Mary Todd Lincoln House
- [ ] 43. share silence with a monk
- [ ] 44. eat a slice of Derby-Pie®

- ☐ 45. visit the Creation Museum with your family
- ☐ 46. spot a celebrity
- ☐ 47. feed the ducks at Noble Park
- ☐ 48. go barhopping with friends at Fourth Street Live
- ☐ 49. visit the home of Henry Clay
- ☐ 50. see a ghost at Bobby Mackey's Music World
- ☐ 51. eat beer cheese at Hall's on the River
- ☐ 52. wear a "gettin' lucky in Kentucky" t-shirt
- ☐ 53. watch a show at the Pioneer Playhouse
- ☐ 54. sit inside the Cane Ridge Meeting House
- ☐ 55. swing a bat at the Louisville Slugger Museum
- ☐ 56. camp out at Red River Gorge
- ☐ 57. use the outhouse at Penn's Store
- ☐ 58. spend a few minutes in jail
- ☐ 59. see "the procession that never moves"
- ☐ 60. take a trip on the Bourbon Trail
- ☐ 61. watch a race at the Kentucky Speedway
- ☐ 62. take a ride on the Valley View Ferry
- ☐ 63. visit the Muhammad Ali Museum
- ☐ 64. sleep in a teepee
- ☐ 65. attend the Garrard County Tobacco Cutting Contest
- ☐ 66. enjoy a concert at Renfro Valley

- ☐ 67. savor a Blue Monday cream candy
- ☐ 68. play a round of golf at Valhalla
- ☐ 69. go to a party thrown by Russ Renbarger
- ☐ 70. touch the pillars of Stonehenge
- ☐ 71. spend a day at Newport on the Levee
- ☐ 72. see the Palisades
- ☐ 73. go birdwatching at the Audobon State
- ☐ 74. Enjoy a bourbon ball
- ☐ 75. drive slowly under a covered bridge
- ☐ 76. see the Jefferson Davis monument
- ☐ 77. admire a painting in the Speed Art Museum
- ☐ 78. go kayaking in the Rockcastle River
- ☐ 79. tour a horse farm
- ☐ 80. drive by the Mother Goose House at night
- ☐ 81. become a Kentucky Colonel
- ☐ 82. tour the Toyota plant
- ☐ 83. search for Herry the Hairless Loch Herrington monster
- ☐ 84. make a mint julep
- ☐ 85. visit the world's smallest church
- ☐ 86. pig out at the International Bar-B-Que Festival
- ☐ 87. touch the walls of the Fitchburg Furnace
- ☐ 88. visit the Harland Sanders Cafe and Museum
- ☐ 89. pay your respects at the Vietnam Veterans Memorial
- ☐ 90. climb Pilot Rocks

- ☐ 91. see a movie at the Kentucky Theatre
- ☐ 92. attend the Kentucky State Fair
- ☐ 93. shoot a gun
- ☐ 94. explore the Cumberland Gap
- ☐ 95. buy something that a Kentuckian made
- ☐ 96. get your wings in a flight simulator
- ☐ 97. walk the grounds of Old Fort Harrod
- ☐ 98. see a model t
- ☐ 99. see a bank robbed by Jesse James
- ☐ 100. share a story with the author of this book

add to the list

☐ 101. _____
☐ 102. _____
☐ 103. _____
☐ 104. _____
☐ 105. _____
☐ 106. _____
☐ 107. _____
☐ 108. _____
☐ 109. _____
☐ 110. _____
☐ 111. _____
☐ 112. _____
☐ 113. _____
☐ 114. _____
☐ 115. _____
☐ 116. _____
☐ 117. _____
☐ 118. _____
☐ 119. _____
☐ 120. _____

special thanks

Clarence Gram
James Gram
Molly Rosen
Scott Hall
Kevin Kifer
David Sloan
Kenny Rice
Han Fan
Angie Davis
Marge Crisp
Scott McBrayer
Andrew Moore
Stacey Gillespie
Ralph Davis
Mike McKinney
Pat Orsborne
Misha Curnette
Fred James
Keith Caudill
Jack Pattie
Michael Cruikshank
Wyn Morris
Christine Tahrjan
Rebecca Leach
Jen Stephenson
Chris Aldridge

and to Pamela Holland for her
passion for great quotes

The Kentucky Bucket List

written by

Michael Crisp

book jacket text and "what to expect" text
written by Michael Crisp and David Sloan

REMIX BOOKS

Murder in the Mountains: The Muriel
Baldridge Story

The Making of The Very Worst Thing

REMIX FILMS

The Very Worst Thing

When Happy Met Froggie

Legendary: When Baseball Came
to the Bluegrass

A Cut Above: The Legend of Larry
Roberts

"Life is a song - sing it. Life is a game - play it. Life is a challenge - meet it. Life is a dream - realize it. Life is a sacrifice - offer it. Life is love - enjoy it."

- Sai Baba